Butterfly

By Wendy Perkins

RiverStream Readers
Great Reading • Real Learning

Learn to Read
Frequent repetition of sentence structures, high frequency words, and familiar topics provide ample support for brand new readers. Approximately 100 words.

Read Independently
Repetition is mixed with varied sentence structures and 6 to 8 content words per book are introduced with photo labels and picture glossary supports. Approximately 150 words.

Read to Know More
These books feature a higher text load with additional nonfiction features such as more photos, timelines, and text divided into sections. Approximately 250 words.

Accelerated Reader methodology uses Level A instead of Pre 1. We have chosen to change it for ease of understanding by potential users.

Amicus Readers hardcover editions published by Amicus. P.O. Box 1329, Mankato, Minnesota 56002
www.amicuspublishing.us

Series Editor — Rebecca Glaser
Series Designer — Heather Dreisbach
Photo Researcher — Heather Dreisbach

RiverStream Publishing reprinted by arrangement with Appleseed Editions Ltd.

Printed in the United States of America at Corporate Graphics in North Mankato, Minnesota.

Library of Congress Cataloging-in-Publication Data
Perkins, Wendy, 1957-
 Butterfly / by Wendy Perkins.
  p. cm. – (Amicus Readers. Animal life cycles)
Includes index.
Summary: "Presents the life cycle of a butterfly from egg to adult. Includes time line of life cycle and sequencing activity"–Provided by publisher.
ISBN 978-1-60753-153-1 (library binding)
1. Butterflies–Life cycles–Juvenile literature. I. Title.
QL544.2.P47 2011
595.78'9-dc22
                                        2010035668

1 2 3 4 5 CG 15 14 13 12
RiverStream Publishing—Corporate Graphics, Mankato, MN—112012—1002CGF12

Table of Contents

A Life Cycle

A butterfly starts its life without wings.
It changes as it grows up. It looks different
at each stage of its life cycle.

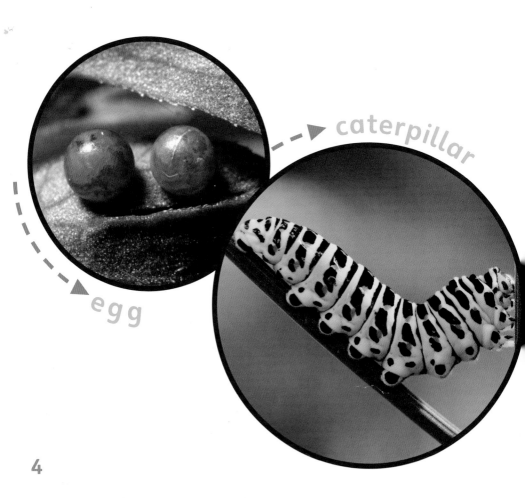

egg

caterpillar

butterfly

chrysalis

Egg

A female butterfly walks on a leaf, tasting it with her feet. She is searching for the right kind of plant to lay her eggs on. Her larvae will eat the leaves when they hatch.

egg

Egg
3 to 7 days

Caterpillar

Butterfly larvae are called caterpillars. A caterpillar's insides grow, but not its skin. The caterpillar molts its old, tight covering about every two to three days. The time between each molt is called an instar.

Egg
3 to 7 days

Caterpillar
10 days or more

After its fifth instar, the caterpillar stops eating. It finds a safe spot on a branch or wall and spins a silk pad to hang from.

silk pad

Pupa

The caterpillar hangs in the shape of a "J" and molts again. Now it is a pupa covered by a chrysalis. The chrysalis may be green or brown.

Egg
3 to 7 days

Caterpillar
10 days or more

Caterpillar changes
into pupa
24 hours

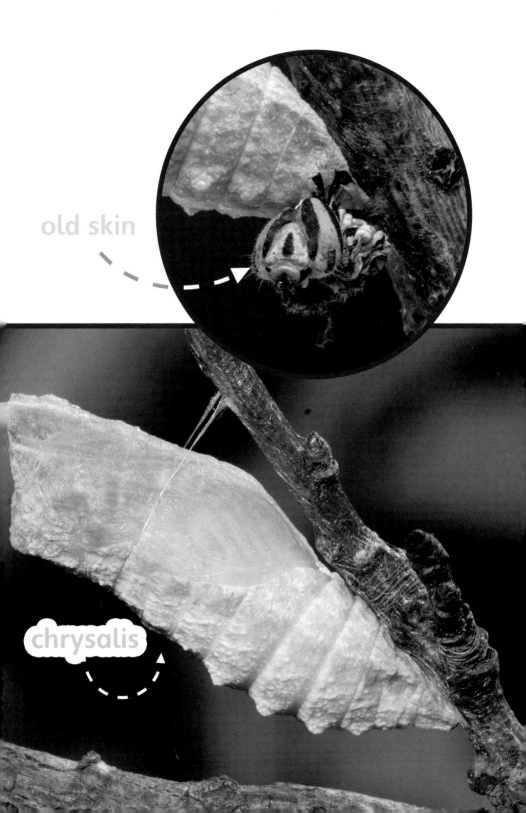

old skin

chrysalis

Inside the chrysalis, the pupa's body is changing. It is growing wings and becoming a butterfly. After a couple of weeks, the chrysalis becomes clear. You can see the butterfly's wing colors.

Egg
3 to 7 days

Caterpillar
10 days or more

Caterpillar changes
into pupa
24 hours

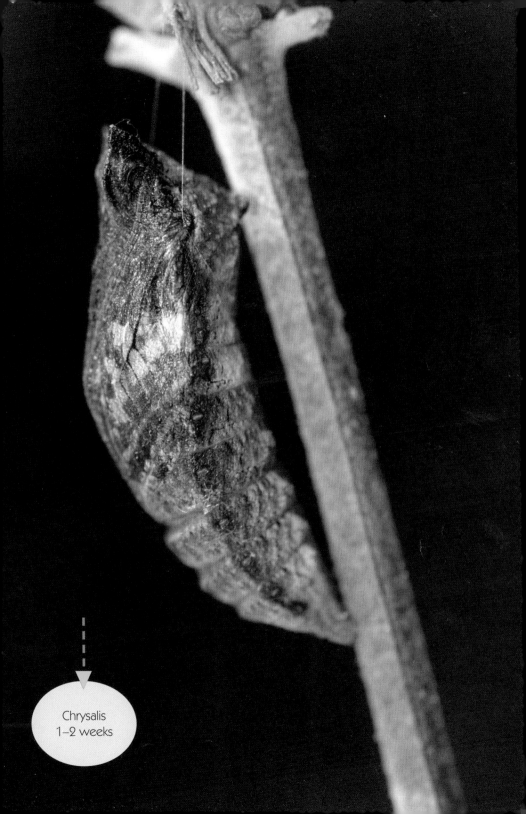

Chrysalis
1–2 weeks

Butterfly

When it is finished changing shape, the butterfly breaks out of its chrysalis. Its wings are folded and damp. After they dry and straighten, the butterfly flutters away.

Egg
3 to 7 days

Caterpillar
10 days or more

Caterpillar changes
into pupa
24 hours

Chrysalis
1–2 weeks

Butterfly hatches
from chrysalis
4 hours

A butterfly is fully grown when it leaves the chrysalis. It drinks nectar, but does not get any bigger. The butterfly lives for just a few weeks. It finds a mate, and the life cycle begins again.

Egg
3 to 7 days

Caterpillar
10 days or more

Caterpillar changes
into pupa
24 hours

Chrysalis
1–2 weeks

Butterfly hatches
from chrysalis
4 hours

Adult butterfly
2–4 weeks

Photo Glossary

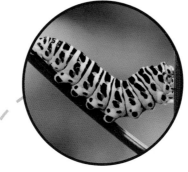

caterpillar
the second stage of a butterfly's life cycle

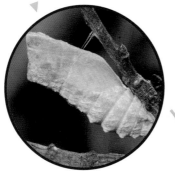

chrysalis
the hard shell that covers the pupa

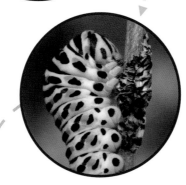

instar
the time when a caterpillar is between moltings

larva
a young insect that hatches from an egg; the plural is larvae

life cycle
the stages of life from
birth to having babies

molt
to shed old skin

nectar
a sweet liquid food
that butterflies get
from flowers

pupa
the third stage of
life of a butterfly

Life Cycle Puzzle

The stages of a butterfly's life are all mixed up.
Can you put them in the right order?

butterfly

eggs on a leaf

caterpillar changes to pupa

butterfly breaks out of chrysalis

chrysalis

caterpillar

Ideas for Parents and Teachers

Children are fascinated by animals, and even more so by life cycles as they grow up themselves. Books 1 through 5 in the RiverStream Readers Level 2 Series let children compare life stages of animals. The books use labels and a photo glossary to introduce new vocabulary. The activity page and time lines reinforce sequencing skills.

Before Reading
- Read the title and ask the children to tell what they know about babies or baby animals.
- Have them talk about whether they've seen butterflies before.
- Look at the picture glossary words. Tell children to watch for them as they read the book.

Read the Book
- "Walk" through the book and look at the photos. Point out the time line showing how long butterflies spend at each stage.
- Ask children to read the book independently.
- Provide support where necessary. Show students how the highlighted words appear in the picture glossary.

After Reading
- Have children do the activity on page 22 and put the stages of the butterfly life cycle in order.
- Compare the life cycle of a butterfly with other animals in the series. Does it have the same number of stages?
- Have the children compare the human life cycle to a butterfly's life cycle. How is it different? How is it the same?

Index

Web Sites

Butterfly School
www.butterflyschool.org

The Butterfly Site
www.thebutterflysite.com

The Children's Butterfly Site
www.kidsbutterfly.org

Zoom Butterflies—Enchanted Learning
www.enchantedlearning.com/subjects/butterfly

Photo Credits
t=top; b=bottom; l=left; r=right; m=middle
Howard Cheek/Dreamstime.com, cover; Framed1/Dreamstime.com, page 1;
Papilio/Alamy, 4l, 6, 22tr; Rasmus Holmboe Dahl/Shutterstock, 4r, 20t, 22br; Jon
McLean/Alamy, 5t, 21bm; Bruno Cavignaux/Photolibrary, 5b, 11, 13t, 20tm,
21b, 22ml, 22bl; Giora Meisler/123rf, 7; Joël Héras/Photolibrary, 9, 20bm;
Stoelwinder Stoelwinder/Photolibrary, 13b, 21tm; Tiziana Bertani/Photolibrary, 15,
16l, 22mr; THOMAS MARENT/MINDEN PICTURES/National Geographic Stock,
16r, 17l, 17r, 22; AnsonLu/iStockphoto, 17t; Jennifer Daley/iStockphoto, 19, 22tl;
Jason S /Shutterstock, 20b; Jens Stolt /Shutterstock, 21t